THE SCHOOLMASTER'S PROGRESS

Caroline M.S. Kirkland

[ZHINGOORA BOOKS]

THE SCHOOLMASTER'S PROGRESS

Master William Horner came to our village to school when he was about eighteen years old: tall, lank, straight-sided, and straight-haired, with a mouth of the most puckered and solemn kind. His figure and movements were those of a puppet cut out of shingle and jerked by a string; and his address corresponded very well with his appearance. Never did that prim mouth give way before a laugh. A faint and misty smile was the widest departure from its propriety, and this unaccustomed disturbance made wrinkles in the flat, skinny cheeks like those in the surface of a lake, after the intrusion of a stone. Master Horner knew well what belonged to the pedagogical character, and that facial solemnity stood high on the list of indispensable qualifications. He had made up his mind before he left his father's house how he would look during the term. He had not planned any smiles (knowing that he must "board round"), and it was not for ordinary occurrences to alter his arrangements; so that when he was betrayed into a relaxation of the muscles, it was "in such a sort" as if he was putting his bread and butter in jeopardy.

Truly he had a grave time that first winter. The rod of power was new to him, and he felt it his "duty" to use it more frequently than might have been thought necessary by those upon whose sense the privilege had palled. Tears and sulky faces, and impotent fists doubled fiercely when his back was turned, were the rewards of his conscientiousness; and the boys—and girls too—were glad when working time came round again, and the master went home to help his father on the farm.

But with the autumn came Master Horner again, dropping among us as quietly as the faded leaves, and awakening at least as much serious reflection. Would he be as self-sacrificing as before, postponing his own ease and comfort to the public good, or would he have become more sedentary, and less fond of circumambulating the school-room with a switch over his shoulder? Many were fain to hope he might have learned to smoke during the summer, an accomplishment which would probably have moderated his energy not a little, and disposed him rather to reverie than to action. But here he was, and all the broader-chested and stouter-armed for his labors in the harvest-field.

Let it not be supposed that Master Horner was of a cruel and ogrish nature—a babe-eater—a Herod—one who delighted in torturing the helpless. Such souls there may be, among those endowed with the awful control of the ferule, but they are rare in the fresh and natural regions we describe. It is, we believe, where young gentlemen are to be crammed for college, that the process of hardening heart and skin together goes on most vigorously. Yet among the uneducated there is so high a respect for bodily strength, that it is necessary for the schoolmaster to show, first of all, that he possesses this inadmissible requisite for his place. The rest is more readily taken for granted. Brains he *may* have—a strong arm he *must* have: so he proves the more important claim first. We must therefore make all due allowance for Master Horner, who could not be expected to overtop his position so far as to discern at once the philosophy of teaching.

He was sadly brow-beaten during his first term of service by a great broad-shouldered lout of some eighteen years or so, who thought he needed a little more "schooling," but at the same time felt quite competent to direct the manner and measure of his attempts.

"You'd ought to begin with large-hand, Joshuay," said Master Horner to this youth.

"What should I want coarse-hand for?" said the disciple, with great contempt; "coarse-hand won't never do me no good. I want a fine-hand copy."

The master looked at the infant giant, and did as he wished, but we say not with what secret resolutions.

At another time, Master Horner, having had a hint from some one more knowing than himself, proposed to his elder scholars to write after dictation, expatiating at the same time quite floridly (the ideas having been supplied by the knowing friend), upon the advantages likely to arise from this practice, and saying, among other things,

"It will help you, when you write letters, to spell the words good."

"Pooh!" said Joshua, "spellin' ain't nothin'; let them that finds the mistakes correct 'em. I'm for every one's havin' a way of their own."

"How dared you be so saucy to the master?" asked one of the little boys, after school.

"Because I could lick him, easy," said the hopeful Joshua, who knew very well why the master did not undertake him on the spot.

Can we wonder that Master Horner determined to make his empire good as far as it went?

A new examination was required on the entrance into a second term, and, with whatever secret trepidation, the master was obliged to submit. Our law prescribes examinations, but forgets to provide for the competency of the examiners; so that few better farces offer than the course of question and answer on these occasions. We know not precisely what were Master Horner's trials; but we have heard of a sharp dispute between the inspectors whether a-n-g-e-l spelt *angle* or *angel*. *Angle* had it, and the school maintained that pronunciation ever after. Master Horner passed, and he was requested to draw up the certificate for the inspectors to sign, as one had left his spectacles at home, and the other had a bad cold, so that it was not convenient for either to write more than his name. Master Homer's exhibition of learning on this occasion did not reach us, but we know that it must have been considerable, since he stood the ordeal.

"What is orthography?" said an inspector once, in our presence.

The candidate writhed a good deal, studied the beams overhead and the chickens out of the window, and then replied,

"It is so long since I learnt the first part of the spelling-book, that I can't justly answer that question. But if I could just look it over, I guess I could."

Our schoolmaster entered upon his second term with new courage and invigorated authority. Twice certified, who should dare doubt his competency? Even Joshua was civil, and lesser louts of course obsequious; though the girls took more liberties, for they feel even at that early age, that influence is stronger than strength.

Could a young schoolmaster think of feruling a girl with her hair in ringlets and a gold ring on her finger? Impossible—and the immunity extended to all the little sisters and cousins; and there were enough large girls to protect all the feminine part of the school. With the boys Master Horner still had many a battle, and whether with a view to this, or as an economical ruse, he never wore his coat in school, saying it was too warm. Perhaps it was an astute attention to the prejudices of his employers, who love no man that does not earn his living by the sweat of his brow. The shirt-sleeves gave the idea of a manual-labor school in one sense at least. It was evident that the master worked, and that afforded a probability that the scholars worked too.

Master Horner's success was most triumphant that winter. A year's growth had improved his outward man exceedingly, filling out the limbs so that they did not remind you so forcibly of a young colt's, and supplying the cheeks with the flesh and blood so necessary where mustaches were not worn. Experience had given him a degree of confidence, and confidence gave him power. In short, people said the master had waked up; and so he had. He actually set about reading for improvement; and although at the end of the term he could not quite make out from his historical studies which side Hannibal was on, yet this is readily explained by the fact that he boarded round, and was obliged to read generally by firelight, surrounded by ungoverned children.

After this, Master Horner made his own bargain. When schooltime came round with the following autumn, and the teacher presented himself for a third examination, such a test was pronounced no longer necessary; and the district consented to engage him at the astounding rate of sixteen dollars a month, with the understanding that he was to have a fixed home, provided he was willing to allow a dollar a week for it. Master Horner bethought him of the successive "killing-times," and consequent doughnuts of the twenty families in which he had sojourned the years before, and consented to the exaction.

Behold our friend now as high as district teacher can ever hope to be—his scholarship established, his home stationary and not revolving, and the good behavior of the community insured by the fact that he, being of age, had now a farm to retire upon in case of any disgust.

Master Horner was at once the preëminent beau of the neighborhood, spite of the prejudice against learning. He brushed his hair straight up in front, and wore a sky-blue ribbon for a guard to his silver watch, and walked as if the tall heels of his blunt boots were egg-shells and not leather. Yet he was far from neglecting the duties of his place. He was beau only on Sundays and holidays; very schoolmaster the rest of the time.

It was at a "spelling-school" that Master Horner first met the educated eyes of Miss Harriet Bangle, a young lady visiting the Engleharts in our neighborhood. She was from one of the towns in Western New York, and had brought with her a variety of city airs and graces somewhat caricatured, set off with year-old French fashions much travestied. Whether she had been sent out to the new country to try, somewhat late, a rustic chance for an establishment, or whether her company had been found rather trying at home, we cannot say. The view which she was at some pains to make understood was, that her friends had contrived this method of keeping her out of the way of a desperate lover whose addresses were not acceptable to them.

If it should seem surprising that so high-bred a visitor should be sojourning in the wild woods, it must be remembered that more than one celebrated Englishman and not a few distinguished Americans have farmer brothers in the western country, no whit less rustic in their exterior and manner of life than the plainest of their neighbors. When these are visited by their refined kinsfolk, we of the woods catch glimpses of the gay world, or think we do.

That   great   medicine   hath
  With its tinct gilded—

many a vulgarism to the satisfaction of wiser heads than ours.

Miss Bangle's manner bespoke for her that high consideration which she felt to be her due. Yet she condescended to be amused by the rustics and their awkward attempts at gaiety and elegance; and, to say truth, few of the village merry-makings escaped her, though she wore always the air of great superiority.

The spelling-school is one of the ordinary winter amusements in the country. It occurs once in a fortnight, or so, and has power to draw out all the young people for miles round, arrayed in their best clothes and their holiday behavior. When all is ready, umpires are elected, and after these have taken the distinguished place usually occupied by the teacher, the young people of the school choose the two best scholars to head the opposing classes. These leaders choose their followers from the mass, each calling a name in turn, until all the spellers are ranked on one side or the other, lining the sides of the room, and all standing. The schoolmaster, standing too, takes his spelling-book, and gives a placid yet awe-inspiring look along the ranks, remarking that he intends to be very impartial, and that he shall give out nothing *that is not in the spelling-book*. For the first half hour or so he chooses common and easy words, that the spirit of the evening may not be damped by the too early thinning of the classes. When a word is missed, the blunderer has to sit down, and be a spectator only for the rest of the evening. At certain intervals, some of the best speakers mount the platform, and "speak a piece," which is generally as declamatory as possible.

The excitement of this scene is equal to that afforded by any city spectacle whatever; and towards the close of the evening, when difficult and unusual words are chosen to confound the small number who still keep the floor, it becomes scarcely less than painful. When perhaps only one or two remain to be puzzled, the master, weary at last of his task, though a favorite one, tries by tricks to put down those whom he cannot overcome in fair fight. If among all the curious, useless, unheard-of words which may be picked out of the spelling-book, he cannot find one which the scholars have not noticed, he gets the last head down by some quip or catch. "Bay" will perhaps be the sound; one scholar spells it "bey," another, "bay," while the master all the time means "ba," which comes within the rule, being *in the spelling-book*.

It was on one of these occasions, as we have said, that Miss Bangle, having come to the spelling-school to get materials for a letter to a female friend, first shone upon Mr. Horner. She was excessively amused by his solemn air and puckered mouth, and set him down at once as fair game. Yet she could not help becoming somewhat interested in the spelling-school, and after it was over found she had not stored up half as many of the schoolmaster's points as she intended, for the benefit of her correspondent.

In the evening's contest a young girl from some few miles' distance, Ellen Kingsbury, the only child of a substantial farmer, had been the very last to sit down, after a prolonged effort on the part of Mr. Horner to puzzle her, for the credit of his own school. She blushed, and smiled, and blushed again, but spelt on, until Mr. Horner's cheeks were crimson with excitement and some touch of shame that he should be baffled at his own weapons. At length, either by accident or design, Ellen missed a word, and sinking into her seat was numbered with the slain.

In the laugh and talk which followed (for with the conclusion of the spelling, all form of a public assembly vanishes), our schoolmaster said so many gallant things to his fair enemy, and appeared so much animated by the excitement of the contest, that Miss Bangle began to look upon him with rather more respect, and to feel somewhat indignant that a little rustic like Ellen should absorb the entire attention of the only beau. She put on, therefore, her most gracious aspect, and mingled in the circle; caused the schoolmaster to be presented to her, and did her best to fascinate him by certain airs and graces which she had found successful elsewhere. What game is too small for the close-woven net of a coquette?

Mr. Horner quitted not the fair Ellen until he had handed her into her father's sleigh; and he then wended his way homewards, never thinking that he ought to have escorted Miss Bangle to her uncle's, though she certainly waited a little while for his return.

We must not follow into particulars the subsequent intercourse of our schoolmaster with the civilized young lady. All that concerns us is the result of Miss Bangle's benevolent designs upon his heart. She tried most sincerely to find its vulnerable spot, meaning no doubt to put Mr. Homer on his guard for the future; and she was unfeignedly surprised to discover that her best efforts were of no avail. She concluded he must have taken a counter-poison, and she was not slow in guessing its source. She had observed the peculiar fire which lighted up his eyes in the presence of Ellen Kingsbury, and she bethought her of a plan which would ensure her some amusement at the expense of these impertinent rustics, though in a manner different somewhat from her original more natural idea of simple coquetry.

A letter was written to Master Horner, purporting to come from Ellen Kingsbury, worded so artfully that the schoolmaster understood at once that it was intended to be a secret communication, though its ostensible object was an inquiry about some ordinary affair. This was laid in Mr. Horner's desk before he came to school, with an intimation that he might leave an answer in a certain spot on the following morning. The bait took at once, for Mr. Horner, honest and true himself, and much smitten with the fair Ellen, was too happy to be circumspect. The answer was duly placed, and as duly carried to Miss Bangle by her accomplice, Joe Englehart, an unlucky pickle who "was always for ill, never for good," and who found no difficulty in obtaining the letter unwatched, since the master was obliged to be in school at nine, and Joe could always linger a few minutes later. This answer being opened and laughed at, Miss Bangle had only to contrive a rejoinder, which being rather more particular in its tone than the original communication, led on yet again the happy schoolmaster, who branched out into sentiment, "taffeta phrases, silken terms precise," talked of hills and dales and rivulets, and the pleasures of friendship, and concluded by entreating a continuance of the correspondence.

Another letter and another, every one more flattering and encouraging than the last, almost turned the sober head of our poor master, and warmed up his heart so effectually that he could scarcely attend to his business. The spelling-schools were remembered, however, and Ellen Kingsbury made one of the merry company; but the latest letter had not forgotten to caution Mr. Horner not to betray the intimacy; so that he was in honor bound to restrict himself to the language of the eyes hard as it was to forbear the single whisper for which he would have given his very dictionary. So, their meeting passed off without the explanation which Miss Bangle began to fear would cut short her benevolent amusement.

The correspondence was resumed with renewed spirit, and carried on until Miss Bangle, though not overburdened with sensitiveness, began to be a little alarmed for the consequences of her malicious pleasantry. She perceived that she herself had turned schoolmistress, and that Master Horner, instead of being merely her dupe, had become her pupil too; for the style of his replies had been constantly improving and the earnest and manly tone which he assumed promised any thing but the quiet, sheepish pocketing of injury and insult, upon which she had counted. In truth, there was something deeper than vanity in the feelings with which he regarded Ellen Kingsbury. The encouragement which he supposed himself to have received, threw down the barrier which his extreme bashfulness would have interposed between himself and any one who possessed charms enough to attract him; and we must excuse him if, in such a case, he did not criticise the mode of encouragement, but rather grasped eagerly the proffered good without a scruple, or one which he would own to himself, as to the propriety with which it was tendered. He was as much in love as a man can be, and the seriousness of real attachment gave both grace and dignity to his once awkward diction.

The evident determination of Mr. Horner to come to the point of asking papa brought Miss Bangle to a very awkward pass. She had expected to return home before matters had proceeded so far, but being obliged to remain some time longer, she was equally afraid to go on and to leave off, a *dénouement* being almost certain to ensue in either case. Things stood thus when it was time to prepare for the grand exhibition which was to close the winter's term.

This is an affair of too much magnitude to be fully described in the small space yet remaining in which to bring out our veracious history. It must be "slubber'd o'er in haste"—its important preliminaries left to the cold imagination of the reader—its fine spirit perhaps evaporating for want of being embodied in words. We can only say that our master, whose school-life was to close with the term, labored as man never before labored in such a cause, resolute to trail a cloud of glory after him when he left us. Not a candlestick nor a curtain that was attainable, either by coaxing or bribery, was left in the village; even the only piano, that frail treasure, was wiled away and placed in one corner of the rickety stage. The most splendid of all the pieces in the *Columbian Orator*, the *American Speaker*, the——but we must not enumerate—in a word, the most astounding and pathetic specimens of eloquence within ken of either teacher or scholars, had been selected for the occasion; and several young ladies and gentlemen, whose academical course had been happily concluded at an earlier period, either at our own institution or at some other, had consented to lend themselves to the parts, and their choicest decorations for the properties, of the dramatic portion of the entertainment.

Among these last was pretty Ellen Kingsbury, who had agreed to personate the Queen of Scots, in the garden scene from Schiller's tragedy of *Mary Stuart*; and this circumstance accidentally afforded Master Horner the opportunity he had so long desired, of seeing his fascinating correspondent without the presence of peering eyes. A dress-rehearsal occupied the afternoon before the day of days, and the pathetic expostulations of the lovely Mary—

> Mine all doth hang—my life—my destiny—
> Upon my words—upon the force of tears!—

aided by the long veil, and the emotion which sympathy brought into Ellen's countenance, proved too much for the enforced prudence of Master Horner. When the rehearsal was over, and the heroes and heroines were to return home, it was found that, by a stroke of witty invention not new in the country, the harness of Mr. Kingsbury's horses had been cut in several places, his whip hidden, his buffalo-skins spread on the ground, and the sleigh turned bottom upwards on them. This afforded an excuse for the master's borrowing a horse and sleigh of somebody, and claiming the privilege of taking Miss Ellen home, while her father returned with only Aunt Sally and a great bag of bran from the mill—companions about equally interesting.

Here, then, was the golden opportunity so long wished for! Here was the power of ascertaining at once what is never quite certain until we have heard it from warm, living lips, whose testimony is strengthened by glances in which the whole soul speaks or—seems to speak. The time was short, for the sleighing was but too fine; and Father Kingsbury, having tied up his harness, and collected his scattered equipment, was driving so close behind that there was no possibility of lingering for a moment. Yet many moments were lost before Mr. Horner, very much in earnest, and all unhackneyed in matters of this sort, could find a word in which to clothe his new-found feelings. The horse seemed to fly—the distance was half past—and at length, in absolute despair of anything better, he blurted out at once what he had determined to avoid—a direct reference to the correspondence.

A game at cross-purposes ensued; exclamations and explanations, and denials and apologies filled up the time which was to have made Master Horner so blest. The light from Mr. Kingsbury's windows shone upon the path, and the whole result of this conference so longed for, was a burst of tears from the perplexed and mortified Ellen, who sprang from Mr. Horner's attempts to detain her, rushed into the house without vouchsafing him a word of adieu, and left him standing, no bad personification of Orpheus, after the last hopeless flitting of his Eurydice.

"Won't you 'light, Master?" said Mr. Kingsbury.

"Yes—no—thank you—good evening," stammered poor Master Horner, so stupefied that even Aunt Sally called him "a dummy."

The horse took the sleigh against the fence, going home, and threw out the master, who scarcely recollected the accident; while to Ellen the issue of this unfortunate drive was a sleepless night and so high a fever in the morning that our village doctor was called to Mr. Kingsbury's before breakfast.

Poor Master Horner's distress may hardly be imagined. Disappointed, bewildered, cut to the quick, yet as much in love as ever, he could only in bitter silence turn over in his thoughts the issue of his cherished dream; now persuading himself that Ellen's denial was the effect of a sudden bashfulness, now inveighing against the fickleness of the sex, as all men do when they are angry with any one woman in particular. But his exhibition must go on in spite of wretchedness; and he went about mechanically, talking of curtains and candles, and music, and attitudes, and pauses, and emphasis, looking like a somnambulist whose "eyes are open but their sense is shut," and often surprising those concerned by the utter unfitness of his answers.

It was almost evening when Mr. Kingsbury, having discovered, through the intervention of the Doctor and Aunt Sally the cause of Ellen's distress, made his appearance before the unhappy eyes of Master Horner, angry, solemn and determined; taking the schoolmaster apart, and requiring, an explanation of his treatment of his daughter. In vain did the perplexed lover ask for time to clear himself, declare his respect for Miss Ellen and his willingness to give every explanation which she might require; the father was not to be put off; and though excessively reluctant, Mr. Horner had no resource but to show the letters which alone could account for his strange discourse to Ellen. He unlocked his desk, slowly and unwillingly, while the old man's impatience was such that he could scarcely forbear thrusting in his own hand to snatch at the papers which were to explain this vexatious mystery. What could equal the utter confusion of Master Horner and the contemptuous anger of the father, when no letters were to be found! Mr. Kingsbury was too passionate to listen to reason, or to reflect for one moment upon the irreproachable good name of the schoolmaster. He went away in inexorable wrath; threatening every practicable visitation of public and private justice upon the head of the offender, whom he accused of having attempted to trick his daughter into an entanglement which should result in his favor.

A doleful exhibition was this last one of our thrice approved and most worthy teacher! Stern necessity and the power of habit enabled him to go through with most of his part, but where was the proud fire which had lighted up his eye on similar occasions before? He sat as one of three judges before whom the unfortunate Robert Emmet was dragged in his shirt-sleeves, by two fierce-looking officials; but the chief judge looked far more like a criminal than did the proper representative. He ought to have personated Othello, but was obliged to excuse himself from raving for "the handkerchief! the handkerchief!" on the rather anomalous plea of a bad cold. *Mary Stuart* being "i' the bond," was anxiously expected by the impatient crowd, and it was with distress amounting to agony that the master was obliged to announce, in person, the necessity of omitting that part of the representation, on account of the illness of one of the young ladies.

Scarcely had the words been uttered, and the speaker hidden his burning face behind the curtain, when Mr. Kingsbury started up in his place amid the throng, to give a public recital of his grievance—no uncommon resort in the new country. He dashed at once to the point; and before some friends who saw the utter impropriety of his proceeding could persuade him to defer his vengeance, he had laid before the assembly—some three hundred people, perhaps—his own statement of the case. He was got out at last, half coaxed, half hustled; and the gentle public only half understanding what had been set forth thus unexpectedly, made quite a pretty row of it. Some clamored loudly for the conclusion of the exercises; others gave utterances in no particularly choice terms to a variety of opinions as to the schoolmaster's proceedings, varying the note occasionally by shouting, "The letters! the letters! why don't you bring out the letters?"

At length, by means of much rapping on the desk by the president of the evening, who was fortunately a "popular" character, order was partially restored; and the favorite scene from Miss More's dialogue of David and Goliath was announced as the closing piece. The sight of little David in a white tunic edged with red tape, with a calico scrip and a very primitive-looking sling; and a huge Goliath decorated with a militia belt and sword, and a spear like a weaver's beam indeed, enchained everybody's attention. Even the peccant schoolmaster and his pretended letters were forgotten, while the sapient Goliath, every time that he raised the spear, in the energy of his declamation, to thump upon the stage, picked away fragments of the low ceiling, which fell conspicuously on his great shock of black hair. At last, with the crowning threat, up went the spear for an astounding thump, and down came a large piece of the ceiling, and with it—a shower of letters.

The confusion that ensued beggars all description. A general scramble took place, and in another moment twenty pairs of eyes, at least, were feasting on the choice phrases lavished upon Mr. Horner. Miss Bangle had sat through the whole previous scene, trembling for herself, although she had, as she supposed, guarded cunningly against exposure. She had needed no prophet to tell her what must be the result of a tête-à-tête between Mr. Horner and Ellen; and the moment she saw them drive off together, she induced her imp to seize the opportunity of abstracting the whole parcel of letters from Mr. Horner's desk; which he did by means of a sort of skill which comes by nature to such goblins; picking the lock by the aid of a crooked nail, as neatly as if he had been born within the shadow of the Tombs.

But magicians sometimes suffer severely from the malice with which they have themselves inspired their familiars. Joe Englehart having been a convenient tool thus far thought it quite time to torment Miss Bangle a little; so, having stolen the letters at her bidding, he hid them on his own account, and no persuasions of hers could induce him to reveal this important secret, which he chose to reserve as a rod in case she refused him some intercession with his father, or some other accommodation, rendered necessary by his mischievous habits.

He had concealed the precious parcels in the unfloored loft above the school-room, a place accessible only by means of a small trap-door without staircase or ladder; and here he meant to have kept them while it suited his purposes, but for the untimely intrusion of the weaver's beam.

Miss Bangle had sat through all, as we have said, thinking the letters safe, yet vowing vengeance against her confederate for not allowing her to secure them by a satisfactory conflagration; and it was not until she heard her own name whispered through the crowd, that she was awakened to her true situation. The sagacity of the low creatures whom she had despised showed them at once that the letters must be hers, since her character had been pretty shrewdly guessed, and the handwriting wore a more practised air than is usual among females in the country. This was first taken for granted, and then spoken of as an acknowledged fact.

The assembly moved like the heavings of a troubled sea. Everybody felt that this was everybody's business. "Put her out!" was heard from more than one rough voice near the door, and this was responded to by loud and angry murmurs from within.

Mr. Englehart, not waiting to inquire into the merits of the case in this scene of confusion, hastened to get his family out as quietly and as quickly as possible, but groans and hisses followed his niece as she hung half-fainting on his arm, quailing completely beneath the instinctive indignation of the rustic public. As she passed out, a yell resounded among the rude boys about the door, and she was lifted into a sleigh, insensible from terror. She disappeared from that evening, and no one knew the time of her final departure for "the east."

Mr. Kingsbury, who is a just man when he is not in a passion, made all the reparation in his power for his harsh and ill-considered attack upon the master; and we believe that functionary did not show any traits of implacability of character. At least he was seen, not many days after, sitting peaceably at tea with Mr. Kingsbury, Aunt Sally, and Miss Ellen; and he has since gone home to build a house upon his farm. And people *do* say, that after a few months more, Ellen will not need Miss Bangle's intervention if she should see fit to correspond with the schoolmaster.

End of the book.